CHANGING TIMES
ANCIENT GREECE

Daily Life

By Stewart Ross

Illustrated by Adam Hook

First published in 2007 by
Compass Point Books
3109 West 50th Street, #115
Minneapolis, MN 55410
Visit Compass Point Books on the Internet at www.compasspointbooks.com
or e-mail your request to custserv@compasspointbooks.com

Library of Congress Cataloging-in-Publication Data
Ross, Stewart.
  Ancient Greece daily life / by Stewart Ross ; illustrations by Adam Hook.
     p. cm. — (Changing times)
  Includes bibliographical references and index.
  ISBN-13: 978-0-7565-2085-4 (library binding)
  ISBN-10: 0-7565-2085-1 (library binding)
1. Greece—Social life and customs—Juvenile literature. I. Hook, Adam. II. Title.
III. Series.
  DF78.R685 2006
  938—dc22   2006027039

Picture Acknowledgments
The publishers would like to thank the following for permission to reproduce
their pictures:
AKG: 6 (John Hios), 12 (Erich Lessing); Art Archive: 9 (Archaeological
Museum, Florence/Dagli Orti), 10 (Kerameikos Museum, Athens/Dagli Orti),
14 (Museo Capitolino, Rome/Dagli Orti), 23 (Acropolis Museum, Athens/
Dagli Orti), 24 (National Archaeological Museum, Athens/Dagli Orti), 26
(Dagli Orti [A]), 28 (Archaeological Museum, Istanbul/Dagli Orti); Bridgeman
Art Library: 17 (Bonhams, London), 18 (Louvre, Paris), 21 (Ashmolean
Museum, Oxford).

Contents

Introduction

Who Were the Ancient Greeks?

The ancient Greeks were a remarkable people who helped lay the foundations of our civilization. They lived in what is now Greece, on the surrounding Mediterranean islands, and on the neighboring coast of Asia Minor.

Ancient Greek civilization began on the island of Crete in about 2000 B.C. Spreading to the mainland, it reached its height during the Classical Period (480–330 B.C.). It lost political independence in about 150 B.C. to the Roman empire but played a major role in shaping Roman life.

The ancient Greeks lived in small, independent city-states. Each one consisted of a city and its surrounding farmland. The most powerful city-states were Attica (Athens) and Laconia (Sparta), a tough soldier-state. The Athenians were rich traders whose influence extended across the Mediterranean Sea. Their city was also a center for the arts and learning. It was home to some of the finest thinkers, writers, and artists the world has ever seen. The Athenians wrote and performed the first plays and developed the idea of democratic government. It is largely because of them that we remember the ancient Greeks today.

Daily Life in Ancient Greece

The city-states of Greece shared the same language and religious beliefs. They also had similar customs, traditions, and attitudes. Even so, daily life varied widely around the Greek world. Slaves lived differently from free citizens, rich from poor, and townspeople from country folk. The lifestyle of a wealthy Athenian woman, for instance, was quite unlike that of a farmer's wife in Thessaly.

During the Classical Period, Athens was by far the most important and wealthy of the city-states. A good deal more is known about it than the other city-states. The Athenians were great writers who left an impressive collection of histories, plays, poems, letters, speeches, and philosophy.

Quotations from the philosophers Plato and Aristotle; the playwrights Aeschylus and Aristophanes; the poets Homer and Pindar; the historians Herodotus, Plutarch, Thucydides, and Xenophon; and the orators Lysias and Demosthenes, help form a picture of daily lives that were as diverse and dynamic as those in any country today.

At Home

Greek homes ranged from small, poorly built homes to neat town houses and elegant villas. Beds, couches, chairs, and a range of storage chests were common furniture. Only the bigger houses had kitchens. Most Greeks did their cooking outside.

> *The whole town should not be laid out in straight lines, but only certain quarters or regions; thus security will be combined with beauty.*
>
> ARISTOTLE, *POLITICS*

In Athens, the walls of ordinary houses were so thin that robbers broke in by digging through them. Most city homes were one story, made of mud bricks, and had three rooms: a bedroom, a living room, and a storeroom. Bigger homes had a second story, approached by a wooden staircase from the outside. The flat roofs served as outdoor bedrooms during the hot summer months. Fancier homes had more rooms, including a kitchen and bathroom, and were sometimes built around a courtyard with a pool and gardens.

The columns that remain of a fine house on the island of Delos marked the edge of an inner courtyard. It was decorated with a colorful mosaic floor.

> *I must tell you, sirs ... my dwelling is on two floors, the upper being equal in space to the lower, with the women's quarters above and the men's below.*
>
> LYSIAS, *ON THE MURDER OF ERATOSTHENES*

quarters: living area

Lysias' remark touches on an interesting feature of traditional Athenian society: the separation of men and women. In the wealthier homes, women lived upstairs, in the *gynaikeia*, and the men lived downstairs. Women ran the household and did indoor activities such as weaving. They were not expected to take jobs and had to be accompanied by reliable male slaves or members of the family if they went out.

Historians believe women in other city-states were not as restricted as the Athenians. Spartan women had much greater freedom, and in the countryside, wives and daughters helped men around the farm.

Athenian women were not allowed to go outside the home unaccompanied and spent much of their time on indoor activities like weaving cloth using woolen or linen threads.

Getting Married

Marriage was immensely important to the ancient Greeks. All young men and women were expected to marry. Girls had little choice in the matter—they did what the men of their family decided. Men who remained single were mocked and criticized.

A teenage bride was adorned for her wedding.

> *Now Leotychides had good reason to hate Demaratus; for Demaratus had robbed him of a bride. He had been engaged to marry ... a daughter of Chilon ... but Demaratus by a bold stroke had got in first, carried off the girl by force, and married her himself.*
>
> HERODOTUS, *THE HISTORIES*

These words show that the bride herself had no say in the matter of marriage, and sometimes brides were not even present at such ceremonies. Marriage was not about love, but about producing legitimate children. Citizens needed to keep their families going so that children and grandchildren (especially males) could honor their dead ancestors. Marriage was considered an important part of their religion.

A vase painting shows a newly married couple processing to their home.

> *She [my wife] came to me when she was not yet fifteen, and had lived previously under diligent supervision in order that she might see and hear as little as possible and ask the fewest possible questions.*
>
> ISCHOMACHUS IN XENOPHON, *OECONOMICA*

Ischomachus' bride was not unusual. Girls usually married a year or two after puberty, at about the age of 15 or 16. Athenian men normally married about five years later, after they had finished their military service. Before marriage, respectable Athenian girls lived mostly in the gynaikeia, and many did not meet their future husbands until the wedding day.

The formal marriage agreement was followed by a round of ceremonies. It was considered lucky to hold the ceremonies during a winter full moon. Sacrifices were made to the gods. The bride was then formally washed, and she made a show of giving up her childhood toys. Finally, the couple enjoyed a special wedding feast before a lively procession led them to their new home.

Children

Although the primary purpose of marriage was to produce legitimate children, Greeks disliked large families because they were expensive. To solve this problem, they left unwanted babies out in the open countryside to die of exposure. They then said the infant had died of natural causes. In Athens, baby girls were more likely to die of exposure than boys. The Spartans were particularly ruthless. All newborn babies were closely examined, then washed in wine. If any physical fault was found or the child reacted violently to the washing, it was killed by exposure.

A relief carving of a young mother sitting with her newborn baby.

Nurse: [M]y dear Orestes, for whom I wore away my life, whom I reared up after I received him from his mother ... and I bore many labors without profit to myself.

AESCHYLUS,
THE LIBATION BEARERS

reared up: raised

Once the decision had been made to keep a baby, it was treated much more kindly. The nurse assigned to care for a child was often devoted. After a child was born, a string of ceremonies was held, ending with a special banquet when the child was officially named. Friends and relatives brought presents, especially charms to bring good luck.

I bore many labors without profit to myself.

Athenian boys played with a hoop and a hobbyhorse.

> He is clever by nature ... from his earliest years, when he was a little fellow only so big, he was want to form houses and carve ships within-doors, and make little wagons out of leather.
>
> ARISTOPHANES, CLOUDS

Wealthy families employed a nurse—normally a slave—to look after young children. Sometimes, if the mother did not want to feed the baby herself, a wet nurse fed the baby with her own milk.

From an early age, Athenian boys and girls were brought up differently. Boys were encouraged to be as lively as possible. Girls would probably not have been given the same opportunities to play. Sparta was different. Here children of both sexes were encouraged to exercise a great deal to strengthen their growing bodies.

Fun and Games

The Greeks certainly knew how to enjoy themselves. Children, especially boys, had all kinds of toys. These ranged from hoops and marbles to wheeled carts. Dolls were made of wood, clay, or cloth. Children also played with knucklebones that were thrown into the air and caught in a game of chance, like jacks.

[W]e are not speaking of education in this narrower sense, but other education in virtue from youth upwards, which makes a man eagerly pursue the ideal perfection of citizenship, and teaches him how rightly to rule and how to obey.

PLATO, *LAWS*

virtue: character

Serious-minded Greeks, such as the philosopher Plato, did not think that playing for amusement was good enough. He wanted all games to teach children something. Music, for example, taught harmony and balance, and sports developed a boy's body so that as an adult he would make a good hunter or soldier.

A fifth-century B.C. pottery doll originally had movable arms as well as legs.

When they grew up, Greeks continued to enjoy sports. Indeed, one of their greatest accomplishments was the idea of an international sports meeting. The most famous, held every four years from 776 B.C., is the Olympic Games. After a gap of more than 1,500 years, they were restarted in 1896 and are still held today.

> *In the foot-race the best was Oionos, Likymnios' son, who ran a straight stretch on his feet.*
> PINDAR, *ODES, OLYMPIAN* X

Oionos' sprinting made him a hero, which is why the poet Pindar remembered him. Running was by no means the only event at a sports meeting. These meetings also included, among other activities, horse and chariot racing, wrestling, boxing, long-distance running, the long jump, and discus and javelin throwing. Separate games were held for women.

The Greeks did not organize games just for enjoyment. Sports kept them fit, but more importantly, they were also a way

Male athletes competed in the nude. Greek javelins were about as long as a man's height. They had a loop of leather halfway up their length to make the thrower's grip more secure.

of honoring a deity. The games were therefore a religious festival as well as a sporting festival. The Olympic Games, for instance, were held in honor of Zeus, the king of the gods.

Education and Training

Education was mostly for male citizens. There were exceptions, though. Some slaves learned enough to become doctors, and a few Athenian women were able to hold their own in intellectual discussions. Furthermore, there was a vast difference between the education system of Athens and that of its rival Sparta.

> [S]ee whether you think that any man who has knowledge ever would wish to have the choice of saying or doing more than another man who has knowledge.
>
> PLATO, *THE REPUBLIC*

The philosopher Plato (428–348 B.C.) helped lay the foundations of Western thought.

Plato promoted the idea that education was valuable and should be required. In Athens, however, there was no guarantee that a citizen would be well-educated. All depended on the parents, who had to pay for schooling.

Boys started school at about age 7, going off each day to the house of their schoolmaster, where the lessons were given. The main subjects were reading, writing, and music. Memorization was an important part of lessons, and pupils were whipped for doing poorly. Games took place after school. Getting out onto the sports field at the end of the day must have been quite a relief.

An Athenian student, seated in class, wrote on a wooden tablet.

> *Reading and writing they gave them [Spartan boys], just enough to see their turn; their chief care was to ... teach them to endure pain and conquer in battle.*
>
> PLUTARCH, *LIFE OF LYCURGUS*

Spartan education was much different from the education in other city-states. Its purpose was to maintain a powerful citizen army. Boys, taken from their families at the age of 7, were raised by the government. They had their heads shaved, slept in dormitories, and had only one item of clothing.

Month after month of endurance training, severe punishment, and endless physical activity made the Spartans the toughest people in Greece. Men who wished to be a part of the secret police (Krypteia) were sent to the countryside alone, armed only with a knife, and instructed to kill any peasant farmer (helot) they encountered in the night.

15

Clothing

The ancient Greeks made do with far fewer clothes than today. All items were handmade from natural products such as wool, linen, and leather and colored with natural dyes. Fashion changed less quickly than today. Also, the Greeks often worked or participated in sports wearing no clothes at all.

Euelpides: I thought it was dawn and set out for Halimus. I had hardly got beyond the walls, when a footpad struck me in the back with his bludgeon; down I went and wanted to shout, but he had already made off with my mantle.

ARISTOPHANES, *THE BIRDS*

footpad: thief, mugger
bludgeon: club
mantle: cloak

A simple article of clothing such as a cloak was precious. Cloaks were carried only in cold weather. The basic item of male dress was a wool tunic, known as an *exomis* when fastened over one shoulder or a *chiton* when it covered both shoulders. Women dressed in a similar loose-fitting garment called a *peplos*. Those who could afford them wore leather sandals, which were removed to go indoors.

A Greek man wore sandals and a practical exomis. In cold weather men also wore heavy woolen cloaks.

he had already made off with my mantle.

A statuette features a woman wearing a peplos. It has been gathered at the waist with a belt to give it the looser appearance that was fashionable in the fourth century B.C.

[I]t is only lately that their rich old men left off the luxury of wearing undergarments of linen, and fastening a knot of their hair with a tie of golden grasshoppers.

THUCYDIDES,
THE HISTORY OF THE PELOPONNESIAN WAR

grasshopper: hair ornament

Thucydides provided an insight into Greek fashion. The basic *chiton* or *peplos* could vary a lot, depending on the material used, its length and color, and the way it was cut. Beards were fashionable throughout the Classical Period. The Athenians wore their hair quite short, while the Spartans left theirs long.

Women's hairstyles varied, although hair was not often cut. Some form of hair band was usually in fashion. Cleanliness, carefully applied makeup, and tasteful jewelry made Athenian women the envy of Greece.

Food and Drink

The basic diet of the ancient Greeks was very healthy, with plenty of fruit and vegetables. Most food was eaten fresh because there was no refrigeration or canning to preserve it. Consequently, the diet changed with the time of year.

[T]hey had all possible good things in the way of supplies—animals for sacrifice, grain, old wines with a fine bouquet, dried grapes, and beans of all sorts.
XENOPHON, *ANABASIS IV*

bouquet: scent

Although the Greeks loved feasting, many philosophers believed in the simple life. Fish and olive oil, with bread, were seen as quite enough to live on. Indeed, many poor Greeks ate little else.

Bread was largely homemade, consisting of flour ground from local grain baked into many different kinds of loaves. There was no shortage of vegetables, especially onions, beans, and garlic, and fruit was eaten in its season. Eggs or cheese provided protein, but meat was expensive and eaten mostly at festival time.

A flute player entertained a group of bakers as they kneaded their dough before baking.

... without water.

his wine neat

> His [Cleomenes'] own countrymen ... deny that his madness was a punishment from heaven; they are convinced ... that he lost his wits because ... he had acquired the habit of drinking his wine neat ... without water.
>
> HERODOTUS, *HISTORIES*

lost his wits: went mad
neat: not watered down

The Greeks drank water and the milk of goats, sheep, and cows, but their favorite drink was wine made from the grapes that grew on the sunny hillsides. As Herodotus explains, the Greeks mixed their wine with water so that it was not too strong.

The main meal of the day was taken in the early evening. This was also the time when the Greeks' famous all-male dinner parties (symposia) began. A symposium started with a hearty meal, accompanied by music, dancing, and other entertainment. After eating their fill, guests settled down on their couches to enjoy hours of lively conversation that usually lasted well into the night.

At ancient Greek dinner parties, the guests did not sit on chairs but reclined on couches.

Farmers, Traders, and Craftsmen

The Greeks believed that everyone had a particular place in society. At the top were the citizens, descended from the families that had set up the city-states. Then came non-Greek resident traders and merchants, known as *metics*. The lowest-ranking group were the slaves. In some states, particularly Sparta, there was a fourth group, known as *helots*. These were native farmers whom the Greeks looked down on and often mistreated.

> *Whoever said that farming is the mother and nurse of all the other arts spoke finely indeed ... when farming goes well, all the other arts also flourish.*
>
> XENOPHON, *OECONOMICA*

The Greeks were famous for their cities, but the cities could not have existed without the surrounding farms. The life of the citizen-farmer was a simple and regular round of plowing, sowing, harvesting crops, and tending flocks of sheep and goats. The most important crops were grain for bread, and olives, which were beaten off the trees with sticks when ripe.

A farmer prepares the soil with a wooden plow, pulled by a team of oxen.

> [I]f the poor, the common people, and the lower classes do well and increase in number, they will increase the power of the democracy.
>
> PSEUDO-XENOPHON,
> THE CONSTITUTION OF ATHENS

Classical Athens was the business heart of the Mediterranean area. The harbors of its port, Piraeus, teemed with ships from far and wide. They came with grain, wood, and rare luxuries such as Oriental silk and African ivory and left with wine, oil, and the city's famous manufactured goods. Much of the trade was with the colonies that the Greeks had established around the Mediterranean.

Athens' crowded streets hummed to the sound of people making things. Carpenters, blacksmiths, armorers, carvers, wheelwrights (wheel makers), coopers (barrel makers), potters, and dozens of other craftsmen worked from dawn to dusk to earn their daily bread.

This fifth-century B.C. vase painting shows a shoemaker cutting leather for a pair of sandals.

Greece was rarely at peace for long. The city-states spent much of the early fifth century B.C. fighting off Persian attacks, and civil war flared regularly between 461 and 404 B.C. The next century saw the campaigns of Greece's greatest soldier, Alexander the Great. The region was occupied by Roman armies in the second century B.C. Not surprisingly, male citizens had to be ready to fight at a moment's notice.

> *Men should not be trained for war with the idea of enslaving those who deserve no such fate. The purpose of such training should be to prevent their own enslavement.*
>
> ARISTOTLE, *POLITICS*

A Greek foot soldier, or hoplite, in action.

Athens' male citizens swore an oath of loyalty to the state, and all of them had to serve in the state's armed forces. At 18, male citizens began two years of military training, after which they were expected to keep fit and ready for action.

In contrast, male Spartans were full-time professional soldiers who lived in barracks and trained continually for the next campaign. This made them the finest, most feared soldiers in all Greece. So that he could concentrate on soldiering, a man's land was farmed for him by his wife and local *helots* (enslaved workers).

help you and your children. wooden wall only shall not fall, but

A fifth-century B.C. carving features oarsmen in a trireme galley.

> *Yet Zeus the all-seeing grants to Athene's prayer that [Athens'] wooden wall only shall not fall, but help you and your children.*
>
> HERODOTUS, *HISTORIES*

The "wooden walls" of Athens were not actual walls but the city's navy. Athens had by far the largest navy in ancient Greece. At its height, the Athenian navy consisted of more than 300 triremes (triple-decker warships), each driven by 170 oars. The rowers were citizens, not slaves.

Triremes had a massive bronze ram in the bow. To attack they raced across the water at great speeds and sank enemy vessels by piercing them below the waterline. The Athenian fleet played a key part in Greece's greatest naval victory: the defeat of the Persians at Salamis in 480 B.C.

Slavery

One aspect of Greek culture was its use of slavery. For a time, the use of slaves was especially strong in Athens. During the Classical Period perhaps one-third of the city's population was enslaved.

A servant girl helped her mistress to dress.

> *Those ... who are as much inferior to others as are the body to the soul and beasts to men, are by nature slaves, and benefit, like all inferiors, from living under the rule of a master.*
>
> ARISTOTLE, *POLITICS*

The Greek philosopher Aristotle defended slavery. He assumed slavery was acceptable because it existed. Most of his contemporaries thought the same way.

A slave was considered a piece of property, like a chair or a goat, that the owner could do with what he wanted. Almost all slaves came from outside Greece, and many were prisoners of war. A slave's way of life depended on who his or her owner was. Household or personal slaves might be very comfortable. A few had good jobs, earning money and eventually gaining their freedom for good service.

against nature.

juggleries, our charms and "laws," which are all

> *[W]hen some man arises with a nature of sufficient force, he shakes off all that we have taught him, bursts his bonds, and breaks free; he tramples underfoot our codes and juggleries, our charms and "laws," which are all against nature.*
>
> CALLICLES IN PLATO'S *GORGIAS*

bursts his bonds: breaks his chains
juggleries, charms: tricks

Plato voices an antislavery argument used by the philosopher Gorgias. Such thinking was rare at the time, although after the Classical Period, slavery became less common. Gorgias is pointing out that slavery is unnatural.

Certainly the way the state treated slaves was against nature. Thousands were forced to work for no wages in the silver mines at Laurion. Poorly fed and constantly whipped, the slaves dug in dangerous tunnels and were left to die when they collapsed from exhaustion.

Digging silver ore deep underground was considered the worst work of all.

Religion

The Greeks believed in many gods and goddesses. These were not particularly sacred, but more like super-powerful, immortal human beings. The principal deities, led by Zeus, king of the gods, were said to live on top of Mount Olympus.

A Greek temple at Segesta, Sicily, was built in the fifth century B.C. It was probably never finished.

Because the deities were said to have human emotions, dealing with them was tricky. They had to be kept happy with prayers and sacrifices and by holding festivals in their honor. For example, the god Apollo was honored by the Pythian Games, held at Delphi every four years.

Hear me, Silverbow! ... If I have ever built a temple to thy pleasure, if I have ever burnt for thee fat slices of bulls or of goats, bestow on me this boon.

CHRYSES PRAYING TO APOLLO IN HOMER'S *ILIAD*

bestow on me: grant me
boon: goodness

Chryses reminded Apollo, a god linked to music, prophesy, and archery, of all the things he has done to please him. The best way to win a god's favor was to make sacrifices. This meant offering the god something valuable.

Simple sacrifices might be fruit, vegetables, or wine. Sacrificing a living animal, like a sheep, goat, or ox, was thought even more effective. The beast was slaughtered on an altar, usually during a festival, and its flesh roasted. Sacrificers ate some of the meat, leaving the rest for the god.

wished to make constant use of it.

> After sending these presents to the Delphians, Croesus a third time consulted the oracle, for having once proved its truthfulness, he wished to make constant use of it.
>
> HERODOTUS, *HISTORIES*

A priestess called for a sign from Apollo in the famous oracle at Delphi.

An oracle was a person through whom a deity foretold the future. The most important oracle was at Delphi, where a priestess answered questions with messages that supposedly came from Apollo. These prophesies were normally worded to have more than one meaning.

Death and Funerals

The elderly were highly respected in ancient Greece. Athens and Sparta even had laws that obliged children to look after their parents. These obligations continued after death, when it was believed the dead traveled to the underworld. The deceased's family had to give their relative an appropriate send-off on this important journey. In unhappy contrast, the death of a slave rarely drew much attention.

A fifth-century B.C. carving features women following a cart bearing a body to its place of burial.

> *"Let us go, horses and chariots and all, to mourn for Patroclus, for that is the honor due to the dead ..."* Then he [Achilles] led the cavalcade three times round the body, all mourning and crying aloud.
>
> HOMER, *THE ILIAD*

cavalcade: procession

Although few Greeks had such a splendid funeral as the warrior Patroclus, all funerals featured colorful rituals and vigorous mourning. The corpse was first anointed with perfumed oils, then laid out with its feet pointing to the door so the spirit could leave easily. A coin was placed in its mouth to pay Charon, the boatman who ferried the dead across the river Styx into the underworld.

all mourning and crying aloud.

the cavalcade three times round the body,

And no woman ... shall be permitted to enter the chamber of the deceased, or to follow the deceased when he is carried to the tomb, except those who are within the degree of children of cousins.

AN ATHENIAN LAW CITED IN DEMOSTHENES' *AGAINST MACARTATUS*

deceased: dead person
within the degree of: related to

Funerals were precisely organized. They took place at night, so the corpse would not defile the streets. With much wailing and weeping, mourners carried the body outside the city walls, where it was either burned or buried in the ground, bringing it nearer the underworld.

The tomb of a wealthy family was marked with a marble slab or statue, some very large and beautifully carved. Afterward, to ensure his or her well-being in the next world, the deceased was remembered and honored at the ancestral shrine within the family home.

The head of the household oversaw a ritual honoring the family's ancestors. Ancestor worship was a strict duty and was said to bring good fortune to the living.

Timeline

All dates are B.C.

c. 2000	A Greek-style civilization appears on the island of Crete.
c. 1400	Greek civilization spreads to Mycenae on mainland Greece.
776	The first recorded Olympic Games take place. Sport is already an important part of Greek life.
c. 750	The Greeks begin setting up colonies around the Mediterranean, spreading the Greek way of life.
c. 750–700	Homer creates his famous poems, the *Iliad* and the *Odyssey*.
c. 705	The Greeks begin building in stone, encouraging the development of architecture and sculpture.
c. 700	The city-state of Athens (Attica) is set up.
c. 650	Classic Greek sculpture appears.
c. 600	"Black figure" vase painting appears.
c. 525	"Red figure" vase painting appears. The playwright Aeschylus is born.
c. 510	Citizens get a greater say in Athens' government, laying the foundations for democracy.
490–479	Greek civilization survives invasion by the Persians.
484	The historian Herodotus is born.
c. 480	The playwright Euripides is born.
461–446	Athens and Sparta fight to dominate Greece. Warfare, always an important part of Greek life, threatens to destroy their power and influence.
c. 460-431	The "golden age" of Athens begins.
c. 460	The famous doctor Hippocrates is born.
c. 450	The playwright Aristophanes is born.
447	The Parthenon and other fine buildings are built.
446	Athens and Sparta agree to a 30-year truce. Greek culture flourishes during the years of peace.
431–404	Athens and Sparta break their truce. Civil war continues, again bringing instability to Greek daily life.
427	The philosopher Plato is born.
404	Athens surrenders to Sparta.
384	The philosopher Aristotle is born.
336–323	Alexander the Great of Macedonia reigns. His conquests spread Greek civilization into Asia.
c. 287	The philosopher/scientist/engineer Archimedes is born.
146	Greece is absorbed into the Roman Empire. The Greek way of life does not disappear, however, and it influences Roman civilization.

Glossary

Difficult words from the quoted material appear beside each quotation panel. This glossary explains words used in the main text.

Aeschylus   A writer of tragic plays.

Apollo   The handsome god of music, prophesy, and archery.

Aristophanes   A writer of comedies.

Aristotle   A scientist and philosopher.

armorer   One who makes armor.

chiton   A male tunic that hangs from both shoulders.

citizen   A privileged member of a city-state whose family has normally lived there for many generations.

city-state   A self-governing city with its surrounding farmland.

deity   A god or goddess.

exomis   A simple tunic for men, worn over one shoulder.

exposure   Leaving a newborn baby outside to die.

gynaikeia   Women's quarters upstairs in a house.

helot   A native inhabitant of Greece.

metic   A foreigner residing in Greece.

Mount Olympus   Legendary home of the gods.

oracle   A priest or priestess able to receive messages from a deity and pass them on to humans in answer to their questions. It is also the place where such future-telling occurs.

philosopher   Someone who tackles abstract questions, such as the meaning of justice.

Piraeus   Athens' port.

sacrifice   Make an offering to a deity, often by killing a valuable animal.

Salamis   A great Greek naval victory over the Persians in 480 B.C.

Styx   The boundary river of the underworld, across which the dead passed by ferry.

symposium   An all-male dinner party.

trireme   A warship powered by a sail and three banks of oars.

underworld   A place far under the earth where the spirits of the dead lived.

villa   A spacious country house, usually with just one story.

Zeus   The king of the gods.

Further Information

Further Reading

Connolly, Peter, and Andrew Solway. *Ancient Greece*. New York: Oxford University Press, 2001.

Doak, Robin. *Thucydides: Ancient Greek Historian*. Minneapolis: Compass Point Books, 2007.

Pearson, Anne. *Ancient Greece*. New York: DK Publishing, 2004.

Roberts, Jennifer T., and Tracy Barrett. *Ancient Greek World*. New York: Oxford University Press, 2004.

Ross, Stewart. *Ancient Greece*. New York: DK Publishing, 2005.

On the Web

For more information on this topic, use FactHound.
1. Go to *www.facthound.com*
2. Type in this book ID: 0756520851
3. Click on the *Fetch It* button.

FactHound will find the best Web sites for you.

Index